Liu Jo Wei
A Chinese Boy on the Goldfields

Written by
Yvonne Horsfield

Liu Jo Wei – A Chinese Boy on the Goldfields © 2023 Yvonne Horsfield.

All rights reserved. No part of this book may be reproduced in any form or by any electronic or mechanical means including information storage and retrieval systems, without permission in writing from the author and publisher. The only exception is by a reviewer, who may quote short excerpts in a review.

This is a work of non-fiction. The events and conversations in this book have been set down to the best of the author's ability, although some names and details may have been changed to protect the privacy of individuals. Every effort has been made to trace or contact all copyright holders. The publishers will be pleased to make good any omissions or rectify any mistakes brought to their attention at the earliest opportunity.

Printed in Australia
Cover design by Shawline Publishing Group Pty Ltd
Illustrations within this book © Garth Horsfield

First Printing: November 2023
Shawline Publishing Group Pty Ltd
www.shawlinepublishing.com.au
Paperback ISBN 978-1-9228-5141-3
Ebook ISBN 978-1-9228-5151-2

*This book is dedicated to the memory of
my uncle Joseph Tong Way (Lau Lung).*

The Story of Liu Jo Wei

Jo Wei lived in the village of Wang Tung with his mother and his grandparents. It was a small village and the family had to work very hard to grow their own food, which was mainly rice. He did have a father, named Liu Xiang Wei, but he could not remember him at all because he had left the village when Jo Wei was only two years old. He had gone far away to another land across the sea called New Gold Mountain, where much gold had been found. Everyone in the family hoped that he would find a lot of gold and return to the village a rich man, so they would never be poor again.

The trouble was that they had been waiting many years and although Liu Xiang Wei sent them as much money as he could, he had not struck it rich enough to come back home. Jo Wei waited and waited until he was nearly eleven years old and had lost all hope

he would ever see his father again when a miracle happened!

Jo Wei's mother had a letter come all the way across the ocean from New Gold Mountain to tell her that his father was coming home on a ship. The journey would take a couple of months.

Jo Wei was very excited, but when he looked at his mother she had a worried look on her face. She told him, "Your father is coming to take us back with him to this New Gold Mountain." Jo Wei did not know whether he should be pleased or sorry. His mother did not seem happy, but he knew she would always do as she was expected to do as a good Chinese wife.

The weeks went by and Jo Wei realised that his grandparents were unhappy. He did not understand why he and his mother should leave the homeland for New Gold Mountain with his father upon his return. Most Chinese would never choose to leave the homeland where they were born. Every day he and his mother would do their share of the work

Liu Jo Wei
A Chinese Boy on the Goldfields

in the paddy fields, planting the rice. His mother worked very hard by his side, but one morning she was unwell and before Jo Wei could catch her, she fell face down in the water at his feet. He called to his grandfather and they carried her between them back to their small hut. His grandmother bathed his mother's face and said that she had a very bad fever. They could not afford to send for the Chinese doctor, so they took turns in sitting by the bed and doing what they could to help.

Unfortunately, hour by hour she gradually became worse and the following morning his grandmother told him, with tears running down her wrinkled, careworn face, that his mother's spirit had flown from this world. Jo Wei was heartbroken to lose his mother at only eleven years of age and saddened that he would soon be meeting a father he did not remember to break the news of her death.

His mother had waited so long for this time, and now her death has cheated them all.

The day came when his father arrived, travelling on foot from the river. A boat had brought him on the final part of his voyage from Hong Kong where his ship had docked. Jo Wei spotted the tall stranger walking towards him, carrying a ta'am across his shoulders laden with belongings. Jo Wei pressed his hands together and bowed respectfully before this man who was his long lost father. His greeting was returned and they were joined by his tearful grandparents who had such bad news to tell.

Liu Xiang Wei had never imagined that such sad news awaited his homecoming and he felt a strong pain of regret that he had returned too late. He realised that he now had a son without a mother to raise on his own and he could not be left behind in the village. The grandparents were growing old and they had already done enough. After a few days of rest, Xiang decided to pay a visit to an orphanage in Hong Kong where young, abandoned girl babies were raised and educated by the German nuns.

His plan was to find a suitable stepmother for Jo Wei by choosing a new wife.

He returned to the village that evening with the news for Jo Wei and his grandparents that he had chosen a suitable young Chinese woman named Mary Song to be his stepmother. She was to come with them both to make a new life at New Gold Mountain. The grandparents were very sad to hear that he still intended to leave the village, because they would not see Jo Wei grow to become a young man.

The day came when they had to say their sad farewells to the grandparents and all in the village of Wang Tung. It was time to board the ship with their few belongings and Jo Wei met Mary Song, his new stepmother, for the first time.

She was very shy and seemed nervous, feeling just the same as he did. She was only eighteen years old and could have been his older sister, he thought.

It was a long and uncomfortable journey and they

both became very badly sea-sick at first, because they were travelling in steerage, below the deck of the ship.

During this time they helped each other and Jo became good friends with Mary. They were both shy in the company of Xiang who was older and still a stranger to them both. At last they neared the end of their sea voyage and they watched as the ship approached the dock of the city of Melbourne!

After they docked and stepped ashore carrying their belongings, both Jo and Mary were wondering what their lives would be like in this strange, new land. Xiang arranged for them to travel by horse and coach to a place called Ballarat, which he said was a famous gold field, discovered in 1851. He explained that they would live in a district called Little Bendigo where he worked in the Presbyterian Chinese Mission Church. He was known there as Reverend John Tong Wei and it was his job to bring the word of God to the Chinese miners and the

market gardeners who grew their vegetable crops down by the creek.

The trip by Cobb and Co. coach took over a day, so they rested overnight in the Border Inn at Bacchus Marsh. At dawn the next day they boarded the coach which had fresh horses for the final leg of their journey to Ballarat. When the coach pulled in to stop at Bath's stables at the rear of Craig's Hotel, Xiang saw a fellow Chinese waving to him with a welcoming smile on his face. It was his friend, Reverend James Chue, who had come to meet them and welcome Jo and Mary to the community. He had arranged for a driver with a horse and carriage to take the weary travellers straight to Xiang's wooden hut in Little Bendigo.

Mary and Jo were so tired that their heads nodded together and they did not see their new surroundings because they had fallen fast asleep. With a jolt, they woke up to see a small, wooden hut situated on the side of a dirt road called

Lofven Street, surrounded by vacant land. Wearily, with stiff limbs, they climbed down from the vehicle. It was a very small building with the barest things inside: a couple of wooden beds, a table and a couple of chairs alongside the fireplace and chimney, but little else. Reverend Chue had kindly seen that it was cleaned and dust free for their arrival.

   Wearily, Mary and Jo stepped inside. They were just so grateful to lay their heads down and within minutes they were both asleep. Xiang woke them early the next morning with some damper and tea he had made for their first home breakfast. It was only then that they looked about them and noticed their strange, new surroundings. They could already see how different their lives were going to be from their village life in China. Outside, the soil had been turned over by the frenzied searching of many miners digging for the surface gold. All of the trees and grass had been removed to create the barest, ugliest landscape, which stretched as far as the eye could see.

Mary realised that she had no close neighbours, but Xiang told her there was a local white family further down the hill and across the road; their name was Stevens. If she needed some help, Xiang said Mrs Stevens was a kind lady who knew about her and Jo Wei coming from China to live there. Because they knew no English, life was going to be very lonely and very hard at first. Xiang was going to be away for long hours each day, visiting many of his Chinese countrymen to preach the word of God to them and invite them to attend his services in the nearby Chinese Mission Church. He hoped that eventually, all the Chinese in Little Bendigo would become Christians like himself, because this was the work he must do as a catechist for Reverend Chue and the Presbyterian church he belonged to.

In the evenings Xiang explained many things to them. Firstly, he said that he was known here as Reverend John Tong Wei because white people could not remember to call him Xiang and could not spell it.

He then began to teach them both some English words so they could make themselves understood. Jo was able to practice with Mary each day.

However, a surprise was about to happen! A loud knocking at the door sounded early one morning and a smiling Chinese face greeted them in the doorway with a large basket full of fresh vegetables in his arms. He bowed respectfully and introduced himself as Fancy John, explaining that he had a plot of land near the creek beside the Mission Church where he grew his crops. He handed the basket across to Jo, saying "Velly good missus for you!" before he broke into speaking Chinese, explaining that he attended the weekly services conducted by John Tong Wei in the wooden church. He soon became a regular, welcome visitor when he called with a fresh supply of vegetables and plenty of conversation in their common native language. Mary and Jo looked forward to these visits.

Jo Wei had not been to school back in China and

his father thought that he should get an education now that he was here, so he was taken to meet the headmaster at Brown Hill State School. It was not that far from Little Bendigo and it would take him less than an hour's walk each way. He started on a Monday and when he arrived, he realised that the other children were staring and laughing at him. They pointed at his clothes and his hair in a long queue, which were both so different to their own appearance. He could not talk to them easily, so he felt scared and totally alone, both in the large classroom and in the school yard. When the bell was rung at the time school ended, Jo quickly made his escape, but not before a group of older children had gathered by the gate to call him rude-sounding names and chant "Ching Chong Chinaman" loudly to his face, with much laughter.

When Jo Wei reached the hut in Lofven Street, he rushed inside and told Mary what a terrible time he'd had that day and refused to return to the school

again. Mary understood what it must have been like for poor Jo and she spoke with Xiang to explain how hard it was for him. Although Xiang was not pleased, he agreed that perhaps it was best to wait until Jo was willing to try again.

How happy Jo was when Mary told him the good news! He ran up Lofven Street to see his friend, Fancy John, and tell him. Fancy John said he needed some help in his garden and invited Jo to come and help him whenever he could. Because Jo had helped grow the crops back home with his grandparents ever since he could walk, he was happy to do something which would be useful. Perhaps his father still had hopes that Jo would be able to go to school, but Jo had made up his mind. He did not want to be the only Chinese face amongst all the white faces who did not want him there.

Meanwhile, he enjoyed helping sweet Mary whenever he could, by chopping the wood and bringing it in to stack by the fireplace each day.

Jo also carried the water Mary needed for the daily chores and for washing. He was happy to run errands up the road to the general store, practicing the words along the way, so he would not make a mistake. The storekeepers, Mr and Mrs Thompson, became used to his funny speech and did not make fun of him when he visited and he always paid for his goods. They even said things to him such as, "You are a good boy to do the messages for your mother."

One day, Mary asked Jo to make a trip to the general store for a few supplies and as usual he set off up Lofven Street at a quick pace. Before he reached the store, he spotted a group of boys about his own age, pointing at him and talking loudly, with the most unfriendly looks on their faces. He was a little afraid to pass them by, but he knew that Mary was at home waiting for the goods. He did not look at them and as he passed, they stooped and picked up some lumps of white quartz rock. One of the boys called out "Hey, yellow Chink!" as he raised

his arm and threw the rock directly at Jo's head. Jo tried to duck, but the rock hit him right on his forehead above his left eye. When the boys saw that it had connected, they ran for their lives as the blood gushed down poor Jo's face. With his hand over the gaping wound, Jo staggered to the store, where Mr Thompson was shocked to see him wounded so badly.

Quickly, he sent one of his customers to call the doctor, while he sat Jo down and tried to mop up the blood running down his face. "Who did this to you, boy?" he asked. Jo did not know his name, but he remembered his face and said he was in the older grade at Brown Hill State School.

Poor Jo sat until Doctor Benson arrived who said, "That will need a couple of stitches to fix it up." The doctor started on it straight away. Afterwards Mr Thompson took Jo home in his horse and buggy, because he did not think Jo should walk back. When they arrived, Mary was shocked to see poor

Jo's white face and the great bandage over his eye. Jo explained to Mary what had happened and she was very upset. "My fault," she cried, but Jo did not blame her of course.

When Xiang returned home later that evening, he was extremely angry to hear what had happened. "Did you do anything to cause this?" he asked. Jo told him the truth and Xiang said he would report this to the police in Ballarat the next day. True to his word, Xiang made a written report and, because he was known and respected as Reverend John Tong Wei, the police said they were going to investigate this crime and find the boy who did it. It was not long before they had found the culprit and a date was set for the court case to be heard. Although the boy denied he had thrown the stone, the other boys avoided getting into trouble by telling the police that it was him and not them. When the boy appeared in court with his mother, he was judged guilty and a sentence of one month's gaol or payment of £10 was

given. The boy's mother agreed to pay the fine. The local newspaper printed the story and Jo Wei felt that the boy was punished as he deserved.

Eventually, Jo decided that he must change the way he dressed and wore his hair, if he was going to stay permanently in this country New Gold Mountain and go unnoticed by the white people. He knew that he would never feel accepted if he stood out as being so different. He never went back to school, but he had Mary cut off his long queue and he went to the barber for a normal haircut. He asked his father to buy him some Western-style clothes and he burnt all his Chinese clothes. He kept his large straw hat only for when he was helping Fancy John in the market garden. As he grew older, he learnt to sell Fancy John's vegetables and call from house to house, delivering the produce in a horse-drawn cart.

Later, he became a hawker and sold many different goods in the same way. Although he would never be a scholar like his father, he managed to make

an honest living in his new country, which he now called Australia. He worked and saved hard to have his own grocery store. One day he met a nice Australian lady called Irene and she helped him in the shop. Soon they were married and in time they had three Australian-Chinese children who were brought up to be true Australians. They worked hard and, unlike how it was for Jo Wei when he was a boy, he made sure that his children had a very good education and were able to get good jobs when they grew up.

Even though their father could not read the newspaper or write any letters in English, his children were always proud of him and loved to hear the stories of his early life in China. He often reminded them to be proud of how they came to be born in this lucky country as true Australians and as the children of Liu Jo Wei.

Word List

New Gold Mountain – The Chinese description for Australia.

Steerage – The word for the poorest level of accommodation below the deck of a ship.

Chink and Chong – Rude words to insult a Chinese person.

Queue – The long plait of hair that all Chinese men and boys wore. It was a Chinese tradition not to cut it.

Hawker – A person who buys goods to sell to people from door to door like a travelling salesman.

Dock – The port where ships land their passengers after a long journey.

Ta'am – Two large carrying baskets balanced each end of a wooden pole which is worn across the shoulders.

Catechist – A Christian Chinese who works for the church to help other Chinese become Christians also.

NEW (TSIN) 新

GOLD (CHIN) 金

MOUNTAIN (SHAN) 山

About the Author

Yvonne is a retired school teacher with specialised experience working at Sovereign Hill and the Art Gallery of Ballarat as Education Officer over the past 22 years. She has recently completed a PhD to research her Chinese connections with the Tong Way family, covering four generations of their life in Ballarat.

The story is about her uncle Joe who came here from China as a child and it tells of his many difficulties settling into his new life. It provides young readers with understanding and insights into the struggle for acceptance when faced with being so different.

About the Illustrator

Garth has primarily been a figure painter for most of his creative life, though he also enjoys illustrating and producing whimsical sketches, such as for his mother's series of children's books.

Recently completing a Bachelor of Visual Art after a long hiatus, now he paints and draws in his home studio in Ballarat and wishes to focus mainly on art, music and related fields of creativity.

www.ingramcontent.com/pod-product-compliance
Lightning Source LLC
Chambersburg PA
CBHW050736110526
44591CB00003B/41